Dedicated to

Lucy Mardes

a very special new mother

The section in the back of this book designated
ACKOWLEDGMENTS
is hereby made a part of this copyright page.

A Baby Is A Special Blessing

Selected by Karen J. Carroll

Illustrations by Victoria Marshall

The C.R. Gibson Company, Norwalk, Connecticut

MIRACLE OF NEW LIFE

Whispers of Maternity

O, hush, little wild bird, trill softly your song—
The shadows are falling...the day has been long:
All purple and crimson and gold, glow the skies—
And under my heart...another heart lies!

O, hush, sportive west wind, blow soft o'er the lea,
All laden with perfume and summer for me:
Blow lightly and faintly as from Southern skies—
For under my heart...a little heart lies!

O, smile on us, Heaven, bend low to us now—
The seal of your glory, place here on my brow:
For twilight is falling...the tender day dies—
And under my heart...a dearer heart lies!

Marcia Ray

Message from God

When God wants an important thing done in this world or a wrong righted, he goes about it in a very singular way. He doesn't release his thunderbolts or stir up his earthquakes. He simply has a tiny baby born, perhaps in a very humble home, perhaps of a very humble mother. And he puts the idea or purpose into the mother's heart. And she puts it in the baby's mind, and then—God waits. The great events of this world are not battles and elections and earthquakes and thunderbolts. The great events are babies, for each child comes with a message that God is not yet discouraged with man but is still expecting goodwill to become incarnate in each human life.

Edward McDonald

He will be a joy and delight to you, and many will rejoice because of his birth.

Luke 1:14

PREPARATIONS FOR BABY

Teach us how to bring up the child who is to be born.

Judges 13:8

Boy or Girl?

Some folks pray for a boy, and some
   For a golden-haired girl to come.
Some claim to think there is more joy
   Wrapped up in the smile of a little boy,
While others pretend that the silky curls
   And plump pink cheeks of the little girls
Bring more of bliss to the old home place,
   Than a small boy's queer little freckled face.

Now which is better, I couldn't say
   If the Lord should ask me to choose today;
If He should put in a call for me
   And say: "Now what shall your order be,
A boy or girl? I have both in store—
   Which of the two are you waiting for?"
I'd say with one of my broadest grins:
   "Send either one, if it can't be twins."

Edgar A. Guest

OUR BABY IS BORN

We are blessed with a

Date   Time

Place

Weight   lbs.   ozs.

Height   inches

Color of eyes

Color of hair

Our child's name

I prayed for this child, and the Lord has granted me what I
asked of him ....My heart rejoices in the Lord.

I Samuel 1:27, 2:1

You brought me out of the womb; you made me trust in you even at my mother's breast. From birth I was cast upon you; from my mother's womb you have been my God.

Psalms 22:9-10

Maternity

Within the crib that stands beside my bed
  A little form in sweet abandon lies
  And as I bend above with misty eyes
I know how Mary's heart was comforted.

O world of Mothers! blest are we who know
  The ecstasy—the deep God-given thrill
  That Mary felt when all the earth was still
In that Judean starlight long ago!

Anne P.L. Field

FIRST IMPRESSIONS

The New Baby

"How funny and red!"
  That's what they said.
"Why, there's nothing but fuzz
  On top of his head."
And they lifted the covers
  To look at his feet.
"Oh, how tiny and wrinkled
  And red as a beet!"
And I heard them whispering
  Behind my back,
"Did you ever think
  He would look like that,
All wrinkled and red
  Like a baby bird?"
Of course they didn't
  Know that I heard.
But I had to smile
  When the baby was fed
To see how fast
  They lined up by his bed,
And in spite of the fact
  He was wrinkled and thin,
They all begged for a turn
  At holding him.

Osie Hertzler Ziegler

Little Hands

Soft little hands that stray and clutch,
Like fern fronds curl and uncurl bold,
While baby faces lie in such
Close sleep as flowers at night that fold,
What is it you would clasp and hold,
Wandering outstretched with wilful touch?
O fingers small of shell-tipped rose,
How should you know you hold so much?
Two full hearts beating you inclose,
Hopes, fears, prayers, longings, joys, and woes,—
All yours to hold, O little hands!
More, more than wisdom understands
And love, love only knows.

Laurence Binyon

Lord Jesus Christ, our Lord most dear,
As thou was once an infant here,
So give this child of thine, we pray,
Thy grace and blessing day by day.
Thy saving grace on him bestow
That he in thee may live and grow.

Fifteenth-Century Petition

I am the bread of life. He who comes to me will never go hungry, and he who believes in me will never be thirsty.

John 6:35

BABY COMES HOME

Home Today!

There are booties and bottles everywhere,
A feeling of happiness in the air,
Talcum and blankets and a teddy bear.

But who cares if things are in disarray...
What a wonderful happening they convey—
You're bringing your baby home today!

Katherine Nelson Davis

GIFTS

This is the day the Lord has made; let us rejoice and be glad in it.

Psalms 118:24

...and a little child will lead them.

Isaiah 11:6

The Children

They are idols of the hearts and of households;
    They are angels of God in disguise;
The sunlight still sleeps in their tresses,
    His glory still gleams in their eyes;
These truants from home and from heaven—
    They have made me more manly and mild;
And I know now how Jesus could liken
    The Kingdom of God to a child.

Charles M. Dickinson

I love little children and it is not a slight thing when they, who are fresh from God, love us.

Charles Dickens

FIRST TIME AT CHURCH

Jesus said to them, "Let the little children come to me, and do not hinder them, for the kingdom of God belongs to such as these...." And he took the children in his arms, put his hands on them and blessed them.

Mark 10:14, 16

A baby needs the sunshine of his mother's love to develop the sturdy roots of a strong and fertile character.

Janet C. Kaye

I will pour out my Spirit on your offspring.... They will spring up like grass in a meadow, like poplar trees by flowing streams.

Isaiah 44:3, 4

At Day's End

I hold you in my arms before the fire
And tell the fairy tale you love the best,
While winter twilight deepens and the first
White star comes forth to glitter in the west.

So softly do you lie against my heart
I scarcely know if it be child or flower
I cradle, till you stir and draw a breath
Of wonder at the tale. O, blessed hour

That every mother knows when at day's end
She holds her little child, a wistful ache
Commingling with her joy, and dreams a dream
For him and breathes a prayer for his sake!

Adelaide Love

He gathers the lambs in his arms and carries them close to his heart.

Isaiah 40:11

GROWING, GROWING

To a Child Growing Up

Little one,
you belong to yourself and God,
you are not mine;
I am only the port
that looses you into the bay,
the tide that bears you out
on your own adventure.

I am your sealegs,
your swift tack astride the wind;
I teach you the bare mechanics of your craft.

But one day,
in the furor of a squall
or in the awful silence of a calm,
you'll find I'm not beside you at the helm;
and, if I've done my job right,
you will not be alone.

Karen Livingston Raab

OUR CHILD GROWS

And the child grew and became strong; he was filled with wisdom, and the grace of God was upon him.

Luke 2:40

Out of the Leaf-Falls

These are the things to cherish:
  A seed and a dream and a child;
Else must the nations perish,
  And earth fall away to the wild.
These are the things to nourish:
  The budding of trees and youth;
So shall the grown things flourish—
  Manhood and beauty and truth.

Author Unkown

I will sing of the love of the Lord forever; with my mouth I will make your faithfulness known through all generations.

Psalms 89:1

Rocker Full of Love

This cherry rocker: once it held
my grandmother, who cared
to rock her daugher with a song,
who knew love's joy is shared.

My mother soothed me in this chair
with gentle, loving arms;
and told me of the wondrous world,
and kept me safe from harm.

My own small daughter asks to rock.
She chants her homemade rhyme,
so snugly wrapped, in that dear chair,
with love that transcends time.

Virginia Covey Boswell

TREASURED MEMORIES

...his mother treasured all these things in her heart.

Luke 2:51

Dear Lord, make me a blessed mother for this child. Help me to encourage this child to grow and develop in every way that You planned. When I don't understand my child, please give me wisdom; when I am depressed don't let me burden this child with my problems, but fill my heart with gladness; and when I am impatient, help me to remember that a child needs a lot of love and patience to develop fully. And help me, Lord, to love my child as deeply and constantly as You love each of us, for You have entrusted me with a tender and dependent person. Above all, dear Lord, help me to guide this child to find the firm foundation that comes from knowing You as Lord and Saviour.

Karen J. Carroll

Teach me your way, O Lord, and I will walk in your truth.

Psalms 86:11

ACKNOWLEDGEMENTS

The editor and the publisher have made every effort to trace the ownership of all copyrighted material and to secure permission from copyright holders of such material. In the event of any question arising as to the use of any such material, the editor and the publisher, while expressing regret for inadvertent error, will be pleased to make the necessary corrections in future printings. Thanks are due to the following publishers and authors for permission to use the material indicated.

BOSWELL, VIRGINIA COVEY, for "Rocker Full Of Love" copyright © by Virginia Covey Boswell.

CONTEMPORARY BOOKS, INC., for "Boy or Girl?" by Edgar A. Guest, reprinted from *The Collected Verse of Edgar A. Guest.* Copyright © 1934.

RAAB, KAREN LIVINGSTON, for "To A Child Growing Up" by Karen Livingston Raab from *Christian Herald Magazine,* 1980.

ZONDERVAN BIBLE PUBLISHERS, for all Scripture quotations used in this book. It has been taken from the HOLY BIBLE: NEW INTERNATIONAL VERSION. Copyright © 1978 by the International Bible Society. Used by permission of Zondervan Bible Publishers.

Book design by Bonnie Weber

Type set in Brighton